WHY ANSON JONES MATTERS TO TEXAS

By Lynn Peppas

Published in 2014 by The Rosen Publishing Group, Inc.
29 East 21st Street, New York, NY 10010

First Edition

Developed, written, and produced by Digital Discovery Publishing
Editors: Molly Aloian, Wendy Scavuzzo
Design & Production: Katherine Berti
Curriculum & content coordinator: Reagan Miller
Photo research: Crystal Sikkens, Allison Napier
Proofreader: Sarah Cairns

Photo Credits: Corbis: 13 (bottom)
Dallas Historical Society, Texas, USA: 19
Dolph Briscoe Center for American History, Austin, Texas: 10, 13 (top), 24, 26, 27
The Granger Collection, NYC: 4, 25 (bottom)
The Image Works: 18, 22 (bottom)
Litchfield Historical Society: 7
National Library of Medicine: 11
North Wind Picture Archives: 7 (top), 8, 20, 21
The San Jacinto Museum of History, Houston: 22 (top)
Shutterstock: 3, 5, 6, 17 (bottom)
Texas A&M Forest Service: 12
Texas State Library & Archives: cover, 1, 14, 15, 16 (top), 23, 25 (top)
Wikimedia Commons: 9, 16 (bottom left and bottom right), 17, 28, 29
Maps by Digital Discovery Publishing: 5, 6

All websites were live and accurate at the time of printing.

Library of Congress Cataloging-in-Publication Data

Peppas, Lynn.
Why Anson Jones matters to Texas / by Lynn Peppas.
p. cm. – (Texas perspectives)
Includes index.
ISBN 978-1-4777-0911-5 (library binding) – ISBN 978-1-4777-0928-3 (pbk.) – ISBN 978-1-4777-0929-0 (6-pack)
1. Jones, Anson, 1798-1858 – Juvenile literature. 2. Texas – History – Juvenile literature. 3. Texas – Politics and government – Juvenile literature. I. Peppas, Lynn. II. Title.
F389.J6 P47 2013
976.4–dc23

Manufactured in the United States of America

CPSIA Compliance Information: Batch W13PK: For Further Information contact Rosen Publishing, New York, New York at 1-800-237-9932

CONTENTS

1 FROM REPUBLIC TO STATE

On February 19, 1846, Texans gathered for a ceremony on the steps of the old capitol building in Austin, Texas. Dr. Anson Jones, the president of the Republic of Texas, gave a speech and lowered the flag of Texas for the last time. Texas was no longer its own country. It had been annexed by the United States of America.

ARCHITECT OF ANNEXATION

Anson Jones was known as the "Architect of Annexation" because he worked to make Texas part of the United States. Texas won its **independence** from Mexico on April 21, 1836. It became the Republic of Texas and formed its own government. Becoming a new nation was not an easy job. Anson Jones became the president of the Republic of Texas on December 9, 1844. He was the president of Texas when it was annexed by the United States in 1846.

In Austin, Texas, on February 19, 1846, Anson told a crowd:

"The final act in this great drama is performed. The Republic of Texas is no more."

Anson Jones was the last president of the Republic of Texas.

Anson Jones was a master diplomat. A diplomat is a person who **negotiates** with other leaders from different countries to get something done. During Anson's political career, he worked with leaders from the United States, Great Britain, and France.

Texas Perspective

Anson worked toward annexation with Sam Houston, who had been president of the Republic of Texas twice.

ANSON JONES'S TEXAS

2 GROWING UP

Anson Jones was born on January 20, 1798, in Great Barrington, Massachusetts. His parents, Solomon and Sarah Jones, were farmers in Massachusetts. Anson came from a poor family that often moved. He had 12 brothers and sisters. His mother died when he was 19 years old.

SCHOOL DAYS

Anson described himself as a lonely and shy young boy growing up. He went to different schools as a child. One of the schools was taught by his sister Sarah. As he grew older, Anson had to work to help his family. He read and studied whenever he could find the time. Later, he went to night school because he worked with his father during the day.

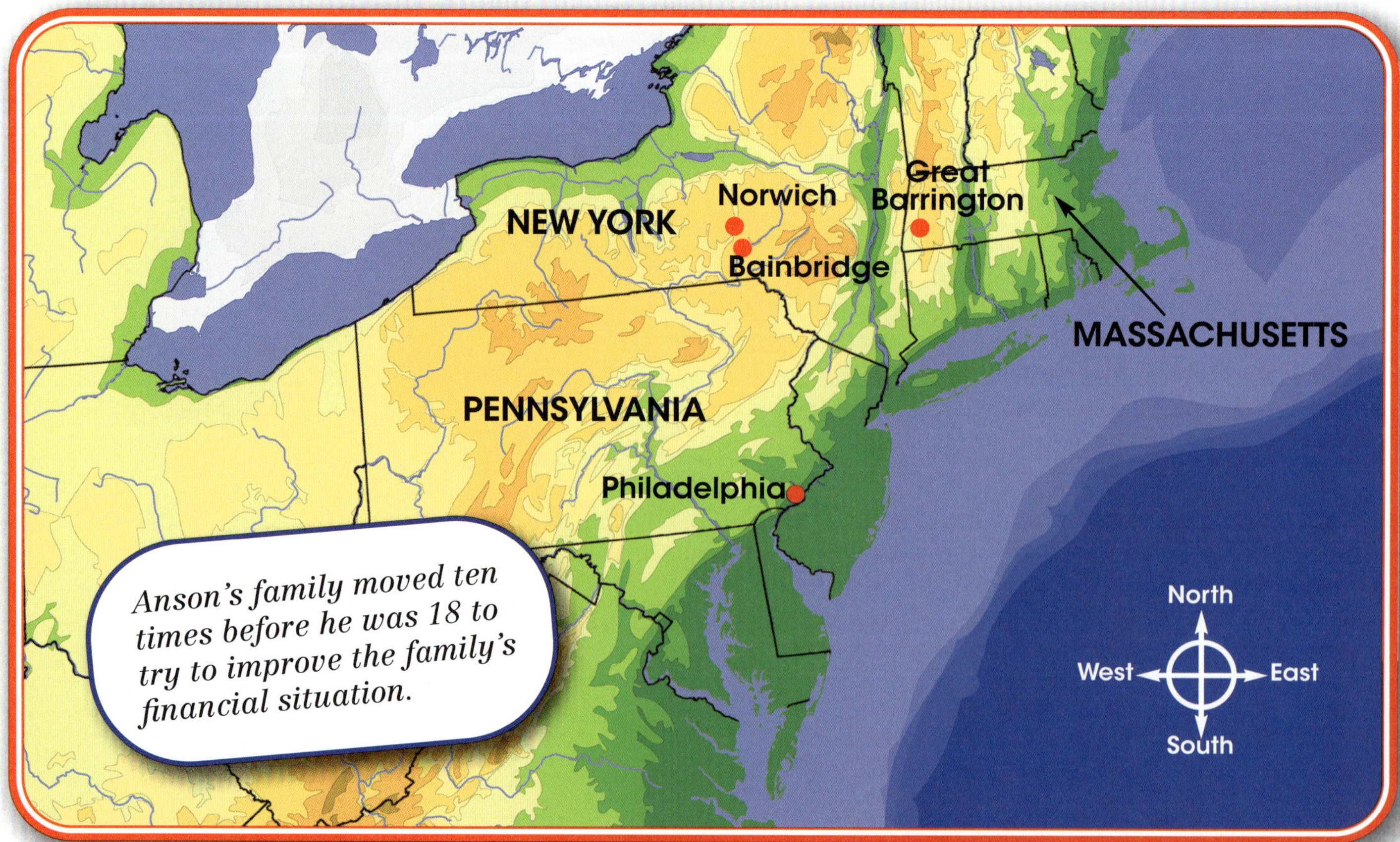

Anson's family moved ten times before he was 18 to try to improve the family's financial situation.

DR. JONES

Anson loved books and reading. He wanted to be a printer when he grew up. After his mother died, though, Anson's father had different ideas for his son's career. He wanted him to study medicine and become a doctor. The family had no money for his education, so Anson paid for part of his schooling by becoming a teacher. He later worked as a clerk in his brother's store. Even though he worked and studied hard, he fell on hard times and was in **debt**.

▲ *When he was young, Anson loved reading books. He dreamed of becomng a printer.*

From Anson's *Private Memoirs*:

"...engaged in teaching a country school, occupying my intervals of leisure in reading such medical or other books as I could borrow, for I was not able to buy any."

The year after his mother died, Anson moved to Litchfield, Connecticut, to live with his three sisters. While in Litchfield, he studied medicine for a year under Dr. Daniel Sheldon (above).

HARD TIMES

Anson finished his studies and earned his license to practice medicine in 1820. He moved to Bainbridge, New York, and set up a doctor's practice but could not make a living at it.

Anson then opened a drugstore in Norwich, New York, but he soon fell on hard times again. He was arrested in Philadelphia for not paying his debts. His goods were taken and sold to help pay the debts. Anson stayed in Philadelphia to open a small medical office, but it also failed. He then went back to teaching.

GOING SOUTH

Anson sailed to South America in the fall of 1824 to open a medical practice in Venezuela. There were very few doctors in Venezuela, and Anson was very successful. He sailed back to Philadelphia in June 1826 and continued his education. Anson earned his medical degree in March 1827.

When Anson's medical practice did not work out in Philadelphia, he went back to teaching.

NEW ORLEANS

Anson was not successful at making a living as a doctor in Philadelphia. He was slowly falling into debt again. He met a **merchant** named Mr. Spear who talked him into moving to New Orleans in 1832. Anson and Spear opened their own store but, once again, the business failed. In the spring of 1833, Anson opened a new doctor's office in New Orleans.

After so many failed attempts at making a living, Anson started to lose all hope that he would ever succeed. He began to live a fast life and gambled what little money he did have left. He lost everything he owned. Anson felt that the only way to get back on track was to leave New Orleans and make a clean start somewhere else.

▲ *Anson was eager to overcome his shyness and meet more people. He joined the Independent Order of Odd Fellows in 1828. The letters in the group's logo stand for friendship, love, and truth.*

Texas Perspective

In 1833, Anson moved to Brazoria, Texas, where he was successful in business, in politics, and in marrying.

BRAZORIA BOUND

Anson met a man named Captain Brown, who suggested he move to Brazoria, Texas, to start his doctor's practice. Anson was unsure about the move. He had heard only bad things about the Texas frontier. He talked to other people about Texas and, in October 1833, he finally decided to make the trip with Captain Brown. Anson did not like Texas at first, and he tried to take the next ship back to New Orleans. Some of the **colonists** in Brazoria convinced him to stay and give Texas a chance. Anson stayed, and he never moved again.

GONE TO TEXAS

In the 1820s, Texas was part of Mexico. At the time, Anglo-American settlers were moving to Texas to receive land and start new lives. New settlers had to become citizens of Mexico and practice the Roman Catholic religion. By 1830, there were thousands of Anglo-American settlers living in Texas. Many also kept their slaves.

In 1824, Texas was joined with another Mexican province called Coahuila. Together they formed the state known as Coahuila y Tejas (left).

A NEW START

Anson still owed thousands of dollars to people in the United States. He moved to Texas with just $17 to his name and about $50 worth of medicines. It was not much to make a fresh start. Anson's luck changed when he moved to Texas, though. Brazoria was not as fancy as other cities Anson had lived in. He found more success as a doctor there than he had in any other location.

In his *Private Memoirs*, Anson writes about his time in Texas:

> *"It is true I have [come across] many hardships ...but, I have succeeded in every thing I attempted and accomplished every thing I undertook."*

CHOLERA EPIDEMIC

In the spring of 1834, Anson was very busy treating patients who were sick from the cholera epidemic. An epidemic is when many people in an area have an illness. Cholera is a disease that causes severe diarrhea and vomiting. It is caused by **contaminated** drinking water and is not **contagious**. Many people in an area get the disease because they all drink the same water. Back in the 1800s, though, the cause of cholera was unknown. There were very few doctors and no medicines to treat it. Many people got well after having cholera, but more than half the people who had the disease died from severe **dehydration**.

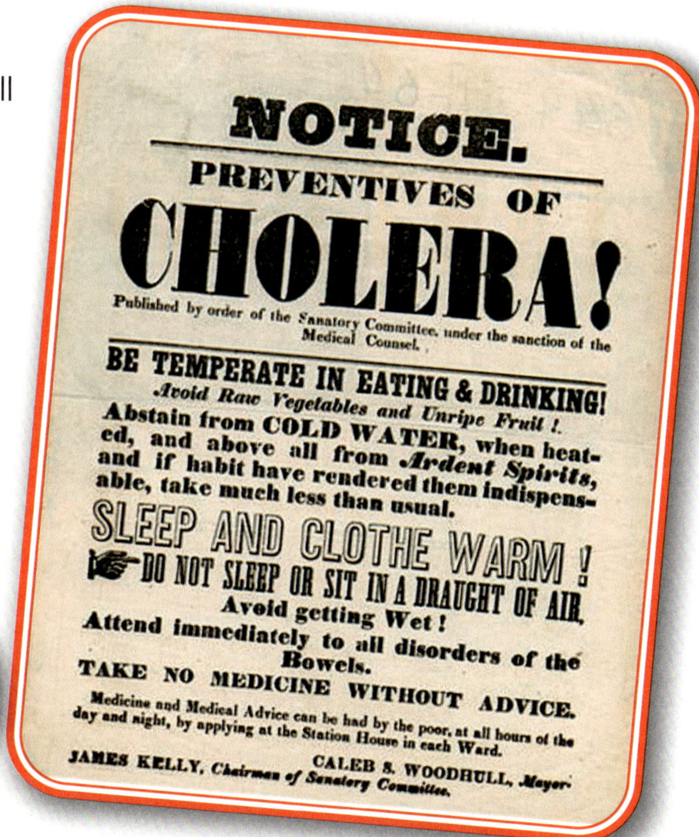

Anson had cholera in the fall of 1834, and he was sick for more than two months. He came very close to death, but he survived.

3 POLITICAL INTERESTS

Before he moved to Texas, Anson Jones had never been interested in having a career in politics. He had always struggled with money. After Anson became a successful doctor, though, he did not have to worry as much about making a living. After Texas became his home, he turned his interests toward the Freemasons and later to politics.

FIRST TEXAS FREEMASONS

In late 1834, Anson became master of the first Freemason's Lodge in Brazoria, Texas. The Freemasons are a very old club for males only. Members meet to discuss and share ideas. The lodge was moved to Houston, Texas, in early 1838. Anson was chosen as grand master of the Freemasons in Texas.

The first meeting of the Texas Masonic Lodge took place under the branches of this live oak in Brazoria County.

TENSION BUILDS

Life was going well for Anson in 1834. His medical practice was well established. He was earning about $5,000 a year, which would be worth more than $130,000 today.

Even though things were going well for Anson, they were not going as well for Texas. Political tensions between Texas and Mexico were getting worse. In 1835, Anglo-American colonists in Texas were unhappy with the Mexican government. The colonists felt their needs were not being met by Mexican politicians. Many began to talk about revolting, or rising up, against the Mexican government.

Dinner to Colonel Austin.

In a speech in Brazoria, Stephen Austin called for a convention of the people of Texas to protest the policies of Mexico.

Anson did not want Texas to go to war with Mexico. He wanted to keep peace for as long as possible. In the summer of 1835, though, it became clear to Anson that this was going to be difficult to do. For that reason, Anson joined a meeting of other Texans who also did not want a **revolution**.

Some Texans joined a group called the Peace Party, while others joined the War Party. Anson wanted peace.

THE CONSULTATION

A **convention** is a meeting of a group of people who wish to work on finding a solution to a difficult situation. **Delegates** were chosen from different areas of Texas. These delegates went to the convention, called the Consultation, to represent, or speak for, the people of the area from which they came. On November 1, 1835, the Consultation met at San Felipe, Texas, to discuss how to bring about peace and a local government for the people of Texas.

Anson traveled to San Felipe for the Consultation. Fierce rainstorms delayed his journey, and he arrived late. In his memoirs, Anson wrote about meeting other important people at the Consultation, such as James Bowie, Sam Houston, and Stephen F. Austin. All these men, including Anson, later played a large part in the upcoming revolution and independence of Texas.

From Anson Jones's *Private Memoirs*:

> ***My impressions of the Consultation...were unfavorable—it was near the close of the session. There appeared to me a plenty of recklessness and selfishness, but little dignity or patriotism [love for one's country]. Still there were some good men there.***

Delegates discussed how best to govern Texas during these public meetings.

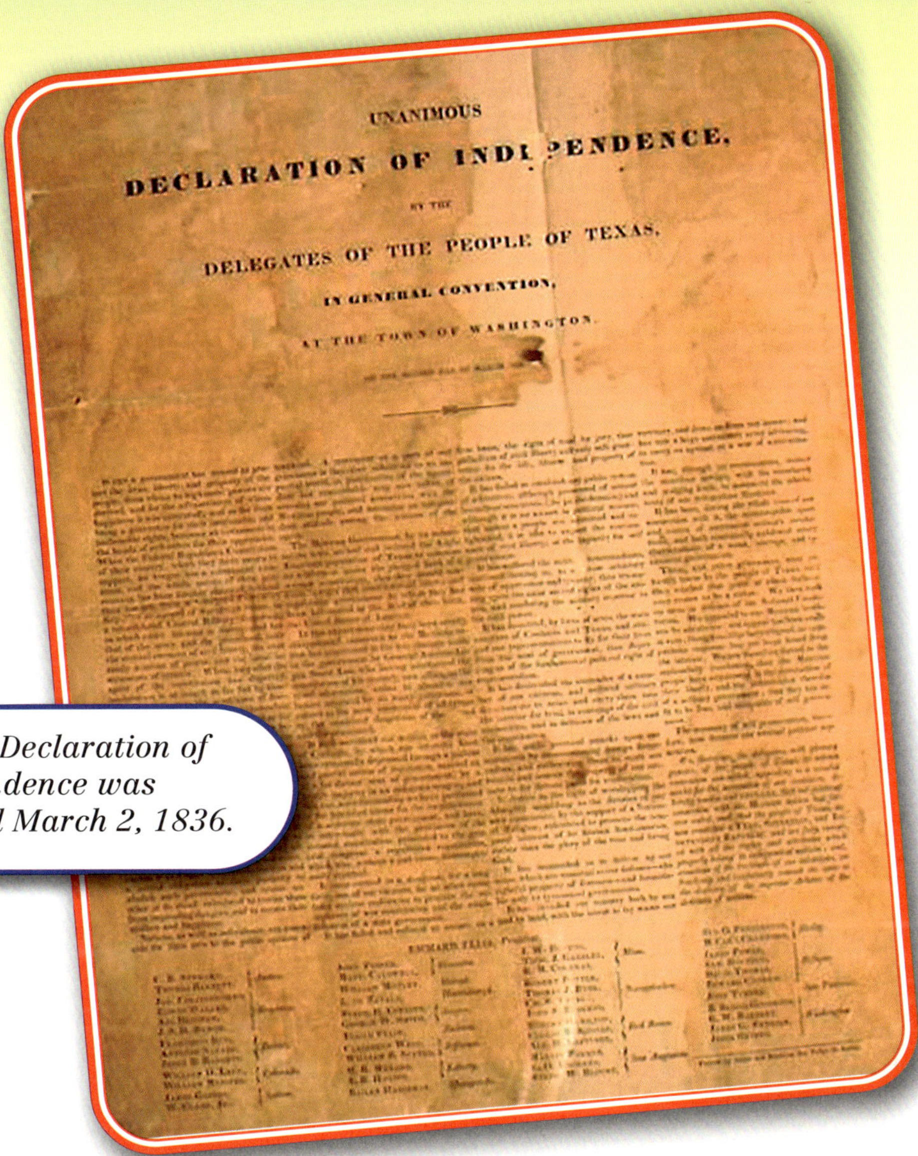

UNANIMOUS

DECLARATION OF INDEPENDENCE,

BY THE

DELEGATES OF THE PEOPLE OF TEXAS,

IN GENERAL CONVENTION,

AT THE TOWN OF WASHINGTON

Texas's Declaration of Independence was adopted March 2, 1836.

DECLARATION OF INDEPENDENCE

Anson came to believe that it was more important for Texas to be independent from Mexico than to maintain peace at all costs. In December 1835, Anson called a public meeting of citizens from Brazoria. Together they drew up **resolutions** called the Columbia Resolutions. These resolutions were to help Texas break away from Mexico and become its own republic. Anson also set up another convention. The convention was to be held on the first Monday in March 1836. At this convention, a new constitution would be planned. Texans elected delegates to send to the convention. Some wanted Anson to represent their area, but he did not want to be a delegate.

STEPHEN F. AUSTIN

Stephen Fuller Austin is often called the Father of Texas. He was the first empresario to settle Anglo-American colonists in Texas in December 1821. In 1834 the Mexican government imprisoned Stephen for almost a year when he presented them with his colonists' **petitions**. Stephen commanded the Texas volunteer army at the beginning of the Texas Revolution. When Texas won its independence, Stephen ran for president of Texas in September 1836, but lost to Sam Houston. Sam made Stephen secretary of state. Stephen died a few months later in December 1836.

JAMES BOWIE

James Bowie was an Anglo American who moved to Texas around 1830. He encouraged Mexicans to apply for land grants in Texas. He then bought the land from the Mexican settlers and soon owned a lot of land in Texas. He fought in the Battle of Nacogdoches, which is considered by some historians to be the battle that started the Texas Revolution. James fought and died in the famous Battle of the Alamo.

James Bowie was well known for his skills with a knife, and his name lives on today in the famous Bowie knife (above).

SAM HOUSTON

Sam Houston was an American lawyer and politician who moved to Texas in December 1832. Sam served as a delegate at the Consultation of 1835. In 1836, he became major general of the Texas army. He led the army to victory at the Battle of San Jacinto on April 21, 1836. This was the battle that ended the Texas Revolution. Texas had won its independence from Mexico.

Winning the Texas Revolution made Sam very popular with most Texans. Sam became the first president of Texas on October 22, 1836.Sam went on to serve another term as president of the Republic of Texas. After Texas became part of the United States, Sam served as a senator and state governor. Sam died in Huntsville, Texas, in 1863.

The city of Houston, Texas, is named after Sam Houston.

4 TEXAS AT WAR!

The constitution of the Republic of Texas was drawn up during the Convention of 1836 in the town of Washington-on-the-Brazos. Delegates to the convention had to pack up on March 17 in a hurry, though. News had arrived that Mexican president Antonio López de Santa Anna and the Mexican army were on their way. The fight for independence for Texas would soon begin again.

ANSON JOINS THE ARMY

In Brazoria, Anson prepared himself for the war he knew would soon take place in Texas. He sent his sister, who had been living with him in Texas, back to New York where she would be safe. Anson heard the tragic news about the Battle of the Alamo in March. He volunteered as a soldier with the second regiment **infantry**. The soldiers were camped near the Brazos River and some became sick with measles and other illnesses. Anson was asked to take the post of company surgeon to care for the sick men. Anson doctored many men back to health.

On April 15, General Sam Houston led the Texas army to Lynchburg. Anson had orders to stay at the camp, but he disobeyed and marched with the army.

▼*Anson took part in the Battle of San Jacinto. During the fighting, he dressed the wounds of injured soldiers. After the battle, he was named assistant surgeon general to the army.*

From Herbert Gambrell's book *Anson Jones: The Last President of Texas*:

> ***"There was no mistaking the [signs that war was coming] when the year 1836 dawned upon Texas... evidence of an early...invasion came with every breeze from the west."***

BATTLE OF SAN JACINTO

The Battle of San Jacinto was the battle that ended the Texas Revolution. It took place near Lynchburg, Texas. The Texas army was outnumbered by the Mexican army. Both armies camped less than 1 mile (1.6 km) away from each other and prepared their men for battle. Around 3:30 in the afternoon on April 21, 1836, General Sam Houston ordered his army to attack. It is a Mexican tradition to take a daily siesta, or afternoon nap. Many of the Mexican soldiers were asleep and very few were prepared for a possible attack. The Mexican army was completely surprised. The battle lasted less than 20 minutes. Hundreds of Mexican soldiers were wounded or killed. General Houston was shot in the ankle during the battle.

The Mexican president, Santa Anna, escaped during the fighting. Sam sent out a search party to find him. They returned a few days later with some Mexican soldiers. They did not know they had also found Santa Anna until a Mexican prisoner greeted one of the captured soldiers as "el presidente," which is Spanish for "the president."

The Battle of San Jacinto was the most important battle ever fought in Texas. It earned Texas independence from Mexico and put the republic on the path toward annexation by the United States.

Mexican president Santa Anna was captured trying to escape during the Battle of San Jacinto. This painting shows Santa Anna surrendering to the wounded Sam Houston.

5 ROAD TO PRESIDENCY

After the Texas Revolution, Anson's feelings toward Texas became more patriotic. He returned to Brazoria to begin his medical practice, but he soon gave it up for a career in politics.

ELECTED TO CONGRESS

Anson's friends encouraged him to run as Brazoria's representative in Texas's Congress. He was elected to the Second Congress of Texas in 1837. Anson did not have a lot of experience as a politician, but he had many good qualities that helped him. Anson was well respected in his community. He was hardworking and paid close attention to details. People thought of him as reasonable, honest, and trustworthy. In Congress, Anson was made chairperson over different committees. A chairperson is a person who leads a group of people. A committee is a group of people who work together to solve the same problem. One of the committees Anson chaired was foreign relations, which is a country's business with other countries.

Houston, Texas, was named the capital of the Republic of Texas. Anson had to travel to Houston for his job. During those trips he lived there.

From Anson Jones's *Private Memoirs*:

"I had 'fought, bled, and died' for the country in the first place, and this had increased my desire to see it prosperous and successful. Habit had accustomed me to reflect more and more upon public matters."

POLITICAL PROMOTION

President Sam Houston trusted Anson more than most other politicians. In 1838, he offered Anson a job as the minister to the United States. At first, Anson felt he could not do the job. Houston urged him to take it though, and Anson agreed.

In Washington, D.C., Anson withdrew, or took back, President Houston's offer to let the United States annex Texas. Anson and Houston hoped that this move would increase trade between Texas and Europe. An increase in trade would make Texas stronger and more attractive to other countries such as Great Britain and the United States.

When Anson Jones was in Washington, D.C., seen below, it looked very different than it does today.

SENATOR JONES

Anson worked in Washington as a representative for Texas for almost one year. In 1839, he was called back to Texas by Mirabeau Lamar, who was the new president of Texas. Anson had grown tired of politics and was planning to give it up. When he returned to Texas, he found out he had been elected as a senator to the Texas Senate. He was to finish the term of another senator who had recently died. He wanted to turn the offer down, but many citizens of Texas urged him to take the position.

AGAINST PRESIDENT LAMAR

Anson accepted the position of senator. He believed that President Lamar and the government of Texas were "sucking the life-blood of the country away." He was determined to do something about it. As a senator, Anson's **opinions** would be heard.

President Lamar sent the Texas Rangers to start wars with Indians living in Texas.

FAMILY MATTERS

Anson served as senator for a total of two years. During that time, he spent time building a house in Austin, Texas. Anson was engaged to a young widow named Mary McCrory. She had been married to a businessman who died just two months after their wedding. Anson and Mary were married on May 17, 1840. The couple later had four children together.

In the spring of 1841, Anson quit politics and moved back to Brazoria with Mary. Anson opened a medical practice but, before long, political life called once again.

SECRETARY OF STATE

When President Lamar's two-year term ended, Sam Houston was elected president once again in December 1841. Houston asked Anson to run as his vice president, but Anson refused. Houston then asked Anson to take the job as secretary of state. This time Anson accepted.

Anson felt that Mirabeau Lamar had almost ruined the Republic of Texas during his term as president. The **economy** was in trouble and the money used in Texas was worthless. Anson hoped that, as secretary of state, he could help make the necessary changes to get the economy back on track. President Houston and Anson thought that the money problem could be solved if Texas joined with another country, such as the United States, Great Britain, or France.

Anson did not like the way President Lamar (above) managed Texas's finances, or money.

Texas Perspective

Anson played a leading role in bringing Texas into the United States.

BRITAIN'S TIES WITH TEXAS

In 1842, Great Britain formally recognized Texas as an independent republic. This meant that they officially treated Texas as its own country, separate from Mexico. Ties to the British were important in Texas. The British trade with Texas brought a lot of money to the new republic. The United States worried that Texas would join with Great Britain. United States president John Tyler began talking once again with Texas president Sam Houston about annexing Texas. The US Senate did not approve of it, though. Texas remained an independent republic during Houston's presidency.

ANNEXATION

What stopped the United States from annexing Texas in the 1840s? One of the main reasons was the issue of **slavery** in the United States. Some Americans believed slavery should be allowed. Other Americans believed slavery should be abolished, or done away with. In the 1840s, there were 26 states in the United States. Slavery was allowed in 13 states. Those states were called slave states. Slavery had been abolished in the other 13 states. Those states were called free states.

In Texas, some of the people owned slaves and many Texans believed slavery should be allowed. The United States had an equal balance of slave states and free states at that time. Bringing Texas into the United States would add one more slave state. That would give the slave states more power over the free states. That is why many Americans and politicians were against bringing Texas into the United States.

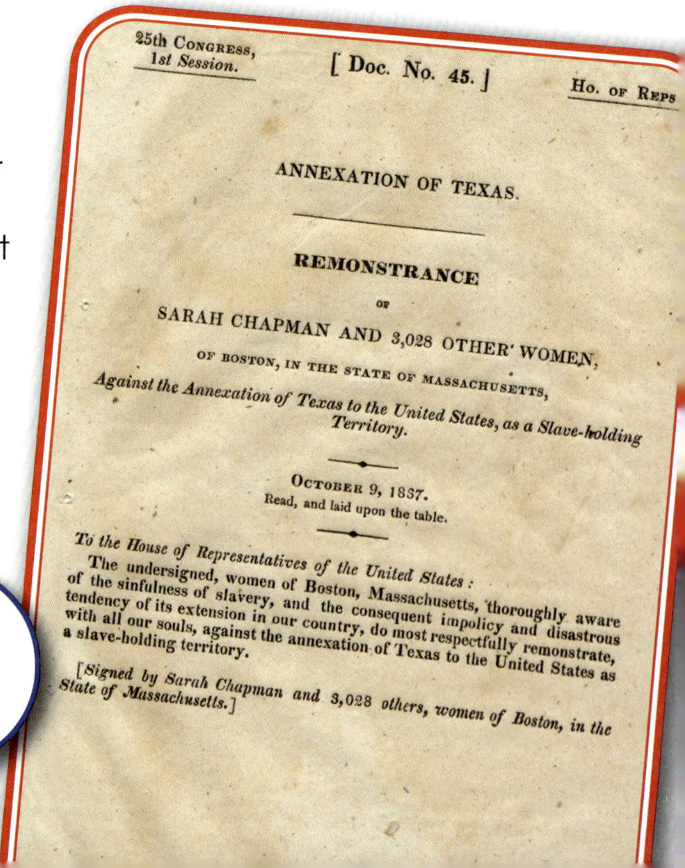

25th Congress, 1st Session. [Doc. No. 45.] Ho. of Reps

ANNEXATION OF TEXAS.

REMONSTRANCE

OF

SARAH CHAPMAN AND 3,028 OTHER WOMEN,

OF BOSTON, IN THE STATE OF MASSACHUSETTS,

Against the Annexation of Texas to the United States, as a Slave-holding Territory.

October 9, 1837.

Read, and laid upon the table.

To the House of Representatives of the United States:

The undersigned, women of Boston, Massachusetts, thoroughly aware of the sinfulness of slavery, and the consequent impolicy and disastrous tendency of its extension in our country, do most respectfully remonstrate, with all our souls, against the annexation of Texas to the United States as a slave-holding territory.

[*Signed by Sarah Chapman and* 3,028 *others, women of Boston, in the State of Massachusetts.*]

In this 1837 petition, more than 3,000 women protested against admitting Texas to the United States as a slaveholding state.

PRESIDENT JONES

Sam Houston's term as president ended in September 1844. Anson Jones then ran for president of the Republic of Texas against General Edward Burleson. Anson won the election and took office on December 9, 1844. During Anson's time as president he did not talk publicly about the United States or any other country annexing Texas. His reason for keeping silent was to keep all three countries, the United States, Great Britain, and France, interested in helping Texas.

Although General Edward Burleson served as President Sam Houston's vice president during his second term, the two men did not like each other.

POLK'S PROMISE TO ANNEX TEXAS

Even though the US Congress had turned down the annexation of Texas several times, many were still interested in seeing it happen. In 1844, US presidential candidate James K. Polk promised to annex Texas if he were elected president. Polk won the election and took office as the 11th president of the United States on March 4, 1845.

During his inaugural address, President Polk spoke of the possibility of annexing Texas. He called it a "peaceful acquisition."

MAKING PEACE WITH MEXICO

After the Texas Revolution had ended, Texas still feared that Mexico would attack and take the country back. Mexico did not officially recognize Texas as an independent country. Anson wanted to make peace with Mexico.

Great Britain and France offered to negotiate a peace deal between Texas and Mexico. Anson believed it was the best chance Texas had to end the threat of future fighting with Mexico. He also felt that it would make the Texas economy stronger.

DEALING WITH THE UNITED STATES

A **treaty** of annexation had been turned down by the US Congress once before. Two-thirds of the US Senate's votes were needed to have a treaty passed by Congress. This time, Polk tried another way to annex Texas. He put the question of the annexation of Texas in a joint resolution, which needed fewer votes than a treaty to pass. The joint resolution was passed by the US Congress in March 1845.

Many Texans had waited years for that day to come. The United States was finally ready to annex Texas. Was Texas ready to be annexed by the United States, though?

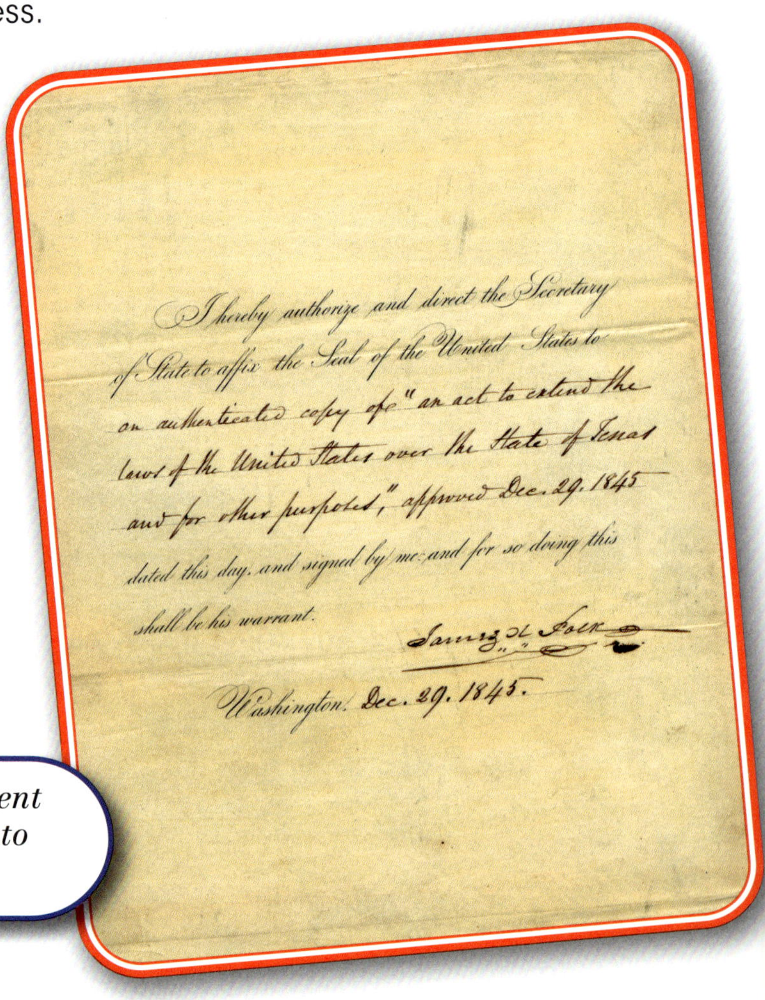
I hereby authorize and direct the Secretary of State to affix the Seal of the United States to an authenticated copy of "an act to extend the laws of the United States over the State of Texas and for other purposes," approved Dec. 29. 1845 dated this day, and signed by me; and for so doing this shall be his warrant.

James K. Polk

Washington. Dec. 29. 1845.

This letter from President Polk admitted Texas into the United States.

BAD DEAL FOR ANSON

Anson had been trying to work out two different deals for Texas with the United States and Great Britain. Neither country knew he was working with the other country at the same time. Anson did not think that both countries would come through with an offer. They did, though, and almost at the same time! Great Britain and France's offer to negotiate a peace treaty came first. Anson said yes to it, but an offer from the United States came in right after it. Anson had a tough decision to make.

Most Texans liked the idea of annexation by the United States. Many did not want a peace deal made with the Europeans. Texans made no effort to hide their dislike for Anson. They got together in large groups and burned effigies, or life-sized figures, of Anson. They even threatened his life.

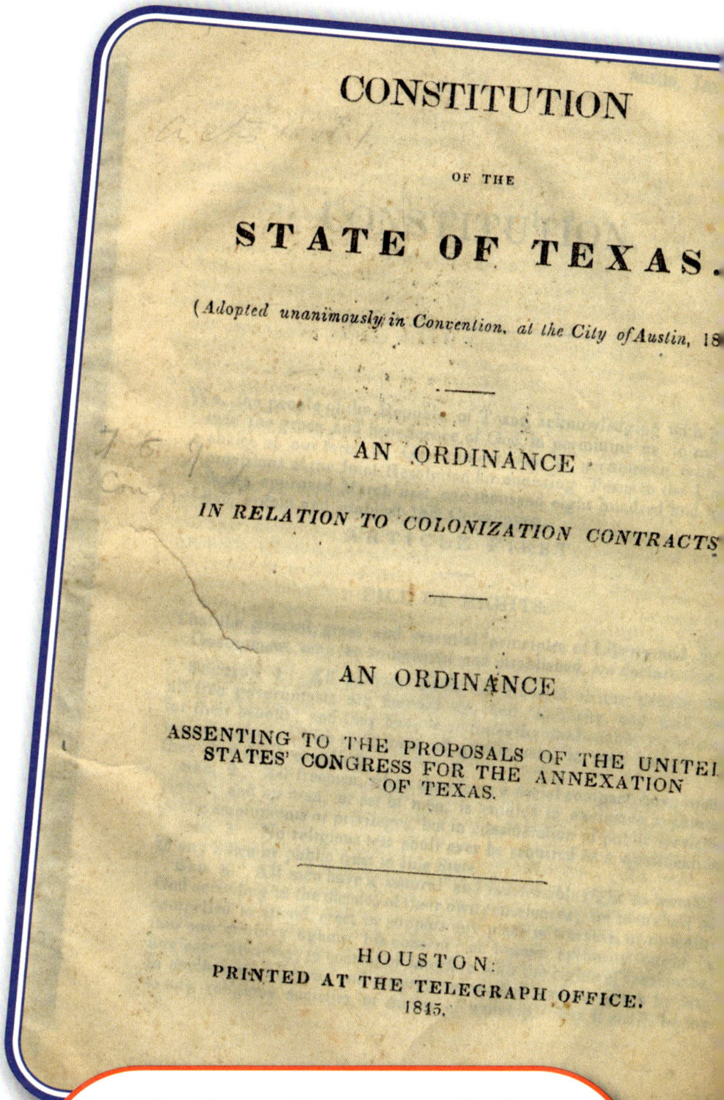

CONSTITUTION

OF THE

STATE OF TEXAS.

(*Adopted unanimously in Convention, at the City of Austin,* 18

AN ORDINANCE

IN RELATION TO COLONIZATION CONTRACTS

AN ORDINANCE

ASSENTING TO THE PROPOSALS OF THE UNITE STATES' CONGRESS FOR THE ANNEXATION OF TEXAS.

HOUSTON:
PRINTED AT THE TELEGRAPH OFFICE.
1845.

The Texas Congress called a convention, during which they wrote a new state constitution. The Texas constitution was accepted by the US Congress.

TEXAS CONGRESS DECIDES

Anson called the Texas Congress into session in June 1845. Congress voted against the peace treaty with Mexico. They voted for annexation by the United States. On December 29, 1845, Texas officially became the 28th state of the United States of America.

PRESIDENT NO MORE

The Texas Congress **censured** Anson Jones. That means they judged him to be wrong in the way he handled Texas. He continued on as president, but he did not take part in important matters. February 19, 1846, was Anson's last day as president of Texas. On that day, an official ceremony took place outside of the capitol building in Austin, Texas. During the ceremony, the Lone Star flag of the Republic of Texas was lowered. In its place, the US flag was raised. Anson gave his final speech as president of the Republic of Texas. Texas was no longer an independent country. It was now part of the United States of America.

Anson retired from politics and lived with his wife, Mary, and their children on their plantation in Washington-on-the-Brazos, Texas. He named the plantation Barrington, after his birthplace.

RETIREMENT AND DEATH

Anson had often struggled financially while working as a politician. He gained a great fortune as a farmer and plantation owner, though. Still, he was not happy. He felt badly that so many Texans had disliked him at the end of his presidency. In 1849, Anson fell off his horse. He badly injured his left arm and could no longer use it. Anson suffered from poor mental health, too. He committed suicide at the age of 59 on January 9, 1858.

From one of Anson Jones's letters:

"I [believe] that when correct information is [spread] in regard to my whole course, the public mind will settle down into proper conclusions, and that my fellow citizens will then judge me rightly."

6 ANSON'S LEGACY

Anson Jones gave many years of his life to make Texas a better place. He worked as a doctor and served as a surgeon in the Texas Revolution. As a politician, he worked as a representative, government minister, senator, secretary of state, and the last president of Texas. Sadly, near the end of his life, he felt as though his contributions were undervalued by the people of Texas.

IN MEMORY OF ANSON JONES

Anson Jones was buried in the Glenwood Cemetery in Houston, Texas. On November 21, 2009, in an official ceremony at the cemetery, the Texas Heritage Society unveiled a historical marker to honor Anson's memory. The marker gives Anson's nickname as "The Architect of Annexation."

The Texas Centennial Commission placed a bronze statue of Anson outside the Jones County Courthouse in Anson, Texas.

The Washington-on-the-Brazos State Historic Site, seen here, is home to the Barrington Living History Farm, which recreates daily life on the farm where Anson lived from 1845 to 1858.

LEAVING A LEGACY

Anson Jones's name lives on today in the Anson Jones Masonic Lodge in Friendswood, Texas, the Anson Jones Memorial Medical Foundation, the Taylor-Jones-Haskell County Medical Society, and numerous awards given to medical professionals in Texas.

The city of Anson, Texas, was named after Anson Jones in 1882. The city is in Jones County, Texas, which is also named after Anson.

LEARNING MORE

BOOKS

Kearby, Mike. *Texas Tales Illustrated: The Revolution*. Fort Worth, TX: Texas Christian University Press, 2011.

Wimberley, John. *Life in the Republic of Texas*. Spotlight on Texas. New York: Rosen Publishing, 2010.

WEBSITES

The Handbook of Texas Online
www.tshaonline.org/handbook/online/articles/fjo42

Texas Beyond History
www.texasbeyondhistory.net

HISTORIC SITES

Texas Parks and Wildlife
www.tpwd.state.tx.us/state-parks/washington-on-the-brazos/barrington-living-history-farm

Washinton-on-the-Brazos State Historic Site
http://www.birthplaceoftexas.com/index.htm

TIMELINE

January 20, 1798 Anson Jones is born in Great Barrington, Massachusetts

1820 Earns license to practice medicine

1824 Moves to Venezuela, in South America, to practice medicine

1831 Becomes grand master of the Independent Order of Odd Fellows in Philadelphia

1833 Opens doctor's practice in New Orleans; moves to Texas

October 2, 1835 Texas Revolution officially begins with the Battle of Gonzales

April 21, 1836 Texas wins independence from Mexico after winning Battle of San Jacinto

1836 Takes part in Battle of San Jacinto; is later made the assistant surgeon general to the Texas army

1837 Becomes first grand master of Freemasons in Texas in December; elected as representative to Texas Congress

June 1838 Becomes Texas's minister to the United States

1839 Becomes senator in Texas Congress

May 17, 1840 Marries Mary McCrory

December 1841 Becomes the Republic of Texas's secretary of state under President Sam Houston's administration

December 9, 1844 Elected the fourth (and last) president of the Republic of Texas

March 1845 United States passes joint resolution allowing the annexation of Texas

December 29, 1845 Texas becomes the 28th state of the United States of America

February 19, 1846 Gives final speech as president of Republic of Texas

January 9, 1858 Dies in Houston, Texas

Texas | Anson Jones

GLOSSARY

annexed (A-nekst) Taken over or added to.
censured (SEN-shurd) Formally disapproved of or blamed for something.
colonists (KAH-luh-nists) People who move to a new place but are still ruled by the leaders of the country from which they came.
constitution (kon-stih-TOO-shun) The basic rules by which a country or a state is governed.
contagious (kun-TAY-jus) Able to be passed on.
contaminated (kun-TA-mih-nayt-ed) Made unusable by adding poisons to it.
convention (kun-VEN-shun) A formal meeting for some special purpose.
debt (DET) Something owed.
dehydration (dee-hy-DRAY-shun) A condition where the body has lost too much water.
delegates (DEH-lih-gets) Representatives elected to attend a political gathering.
economy (ih-KAH-nuh-mee) The way in which a country or a business oversees its supplies and power sources.
independence (in-dih-PEN-dents) Freedom from the control or support of other people.
infantry (IN-fun-tree) The part of an army that fights on foot.
merchant (MER-chunt) Someone who owns a business that sells goods.
negotiates (nih-GOH-shee-aytz) Talks over and arranges terms for an agreement.
opinions (uh-PIN-yunz) Beliefs that are based on what people think rather than what is known to be true.
patriotic (pay-tree-AH-tik) Showing love for one's country
petition (puh-TIH-shun) A formal way to ask for something to be done.
politics (PAH-lih-tiks) The science of governments and elections.
resolutions (reh-zuh-LOO-shunz) Official statements of the ideas of a group, voted on and put to use.
revolution (reh-vuh-LOO-shun) A complete change in government.
slavery (SLAY-vuh-ree) The system of one person "owning" another.
treaty (TREE-tee) An official agreement, signed and agreed upon by each party.

INDEX